Grimoire of
a **Black** Girl

I put a spell on you

And now this world is mine.
Enthralled with my Melanin
Skin kissed by the sun
Soul filled by the Moon.
We are everything in this world.
So, they call us magic.

How else do you explain
The strength

We've endured.
Heartbreak is genetic.

Generations have been broken.
And we're still fixing others.
Generations have been broken.
And we are still fixing Brothers.
Everybody loves our magic.
When it's being used
On everybody but ourselves.
Black Witches
Turned to black bitches.
But we're still providing stitches.
I don't get it.
Why aren't we showered
With the love they're always
Talking about.

Our reign.
Our rain.
They weigh down our crowns
And wonder how we
Have so much power

When our heads are bowed.
This crown is burdened.
And we are the only ones carrying it.
But our strength...not our burdens
makes them angry. Imagine that.

Attempts on our bodies and spirits
Will never stop the things we do.

"It's been 300 hundred years
Right down to the day.
Now the witches are back
There will be hell to pay"

Grimoire of a Black Girl

by
Krystal Kantrell

To my mom,

Princess Ann Tucker-Roberts
I love you, more than everything.

Table of Contents

Acknowledgement

I would like to thank the following people
for helping me navigate this world and recognizing my magic before I
even knew there was even a spark there:

My Mom and Dad
Princess and John Roberts.

My Sisters
Haley, Johnnae, and Ty'keila.

My Family
Aunt Twiggy, Aunt Nita, Aunt Gina, Aunt Sharon, Uncle Cookie, Uncle
Gerald, Uncle Cupid, Kelsi, Tre, Brentley...
and especially my Grandparents Prince and Mattie.

*Mattie, you taught me how to spit fire
and smile with the best of them. I thank you.*

My Friends
Brandis, Kevin, Curtis, Fassett,
Monique, Julia, Tiauna, and Liz.

My Angels
Sister, Aunt Addie, and Devon.

You all don't know it yet, but you're all my coven.
My earth, my water, my wind, my fire, and my spirit.

Preface

Grimoire (/ɡrɪmˈwɑːr/ *grim-WAR*) is a textbook of <u>magic</u>, typically including instructions on how to create magical objects like <u>talismans</u> and <u>amulets</u>, how to perform magical <u>spells</u>, <u>charms</u> and <u>divination</u>, and how to summon or invoke supernatural entities such as <u>angels</u>, <u>spirits</u>, and <u>demons</u>.

I am a sister, I am a daughter, I am a teacher, and I am a lover. As a Black Girl who has been raised in rural towns throughout the south, there are times when I feel like I don't belong anywhere, and there are times when I don't want anything more than what I have at this moment. Whenever I watch the news and/or get on social media to witness how we're currently being treated and how we're all living, I fight for the strength not to lose my sanity. There are so many of us who feel like there's something missing - I write to fill in the blanks. Understand that your feelings are valid, we need to own our feelings, own our anger (We have a lot to be mad about), and use it. Become the witches and the covens that we all need each other to be.

Grimoire of a Black Girl is about me understanding and accepting the fact that I am a Black Girl, and I am Magic. Grimoire is how I've managed to navigate through these different seasons in my life. It has been a saving grace for me ever since Trayvon, and has helped me manage to get through this world after Trayvon. This book is anger, it is love, and it is perseverance. These poems are my spells. I wrote them for us:

For Black Girls who need reassurance
when they feel their magic isn't enough

Chapter 1

Summertime

Hey Black Girl.
As bright as the sun
As dark as the night.
And out of that night.
We are unconquerable.
Right?

We gon' be alright.

We. Me. You. Us.
The sleepless nights,
The endless fights.
Or simple rights.

We gon' be alright.

The strength of a black woman.
Equal to a thousand years of wait.
For a change to come.
Carrying that weight.
Unbowed. Unbroken.
Breaking these chains.
Break free Black Girl.
Save me.

Resistance

Anger so tangible
She made it human
The magical expressions of God herself.
We are the bows that God threw.
Bullets bounce to the beat.
'Knuck If You Buck' is our speak.
Our freedom is showing.
Careful.
We dance through every pain.
Every song is our anthem
Until we pledge to ourselves.
Allegiance to the black bodies.
So filled with lightning
It's a shock, but you're blinded
By our compassion.
Our Grace...we will leave at the altar. This time.
The people will fly again.
You will no longer tread on our wings.
I will never understand
How freedom threatens you.
But I guess
If my freedom relied
On the oppression of others.
I would be scared too.

Finding Myself

What identity can you assume
For your safety?
Where can I go
For my health
Who will do something
For our humanity
We're losing it
Me too.
It's been gone but
I don't know
When it became ok
For people to feel entitled
To my life.
To your life
To our lives
A toast
To the good times
Where we only got stabbed
In our backs.
By America
Now it's guns.
Churches, schools, and clubs.
The new trenches.
A free mind is a dangerous place.
Your body isn't a safe space.

No such thing as a bulletproof vest for our minds.

It was the best of the worst of the times.
What do we do?
Who do we become?
So that we don't die
Because of who we are

The People Are The Crop

I've been walking.
My Soul laid bare
Just like my feet.
On this dirt road
behind my grandma's house.
Holding some eggs
I got out of the chicken coop.
The dog just got loose
And I ain't trippin'
I'm at peace.
I'm in the South.
My aunt lives down there
My uncle over there
And my church is next door.
This street is my village
Fish fry's and funerals
And Black folk
We get the occasional
People that don't belong.
Passing through. Speeding
Through our easy lives
Messing with the winds
Some of us can get blown away
By things that don't belong here.
Black folk.
You can call us dandelions.
We everywhere.
But we stay planted.

Black Girl Magic

Everybody Loves
Our magic when its used on
everyone but us.

My Other Home

South Carolina
Summers taste like Red Velvet
Cake and boiled peanuts.

Black People

Are the heartbeat.
We are the backs
That keep getting
Broken
So others can stand.
We barely have
ground to walk on
But you expect us
To put our faith in you.
The ones who live by
Hands up...go shoot
The ones who
Are the supposed heroes
But only become heroes
When they kill out of fear.
We are the heartbeat
Of this nation.
Beating stronger
After every crucifixion
After every benediction
We are our ancestors prayers
We are our ancestors layers.
They are inside of us
covered, remembered, and protected by
Memories of anger
And sadness.
These people don't know
That we will tear this shit down.
Because
We built it.
I brought you in this
World and I can take you out.
America needs to know
That we ain't playing.
Our ancestors walk with us.
They talk with us.
And we are blessed
To have their strength
To Knuck. To Buck. To Fuck.
This system
All the way up.
If we have to.

Mad Summer

Black Girl.
Sun.
Bright Girl.
You shine so
From the inside.

I feel your anger.

We got a lot to be mad about.
It ain't cool.
But it's cool.

I feel it.

I feel lit.
Why you always so mad.
Expected to be everything
For everybody.
But when it's time to be
Something for me.
You mad.
Why you mad.
When I take time
For myself.
I call it Self Care.
You call it Selfish.
Maddening.

Chapter 2

The Fall

I don't think
there's anything Godly
About a nothing
That's excruciatingly painful.
Where it stems
from the heart
And you can't remember
Whether it broke recently
Or if it's always been that way.
There's nothing Godly about
Realizing that everybody
Doesn't feel empty
Like you do.
That it's not common.
Or that it's more prevalent
Than any other emotion
You've ever been acquainted.
Depression
That old familiar.
Like a black cat
To a witch
My sidekick
Comes with extreme lows
And pain that
Spreads out of my pores
Like smoke billowing
From a California wildfire.
I don't understand
How a God
Could create something
So hauntingly hollow.
Maybe I'm ungodly.
Or maybe
I'm alive.
Barely.

# #

I wonder if Oscar Grant had dreams
He was so passionate about?
That just maybe
He couldn't stomach them
And they had to escape through his back.
Taking his life along for the ride
Caught sleeping on his stomach
I guess he was kissing the ground goodbye
Before he knew what hit him
Or should I say stunned him
Or better yet killed him.
Dreams spilling out his back
No crying over spilt milk
Tell that to a city whose lives have been curdling
Since before they can remember
They should be used to it by now
No crying is allowed over wasted blood
Right?
People should just accept this cause it's the norm
Except it's not normal
Others have been noticing
Brutality rates have been escalating
And cases of policemen escaping
is about equal.

What about the people who couldn't escape them
So, they ended up fleeing life.
It wasn't their fault
The officer accidentally pulled a handgun
Instead of a stun gun.
Black is a target.
The young gun hit bullseye
He got that blue ribbon
It's like that volcano that always wins
Only because it explodes better than the other kids.
There are no lids to cap
This dormant monster
Tensions have been pouring...
And the law has been ignoring
What their purpose is.
A man died because of a "mistake."
These people are no longer complacent
Nor have they ever been.
When this lava hits the fan
All this boiling over is going to start.
The people are gonna be
The earthquake that rocks California
Haven't you seen the tremors before?

Hey Sis

I wish you would've told me.

That the world was your enemy.

Because

I would've fought it for you.

I understand.

Your pain became painless
And I'm not sure if I blame you. But
We could've carried this load together.
I would've carried you.
If you gave me the chance.

I hope you forgive me.

For not feeling your pain.
For not taking it away when it became unbearable.
Your silence is so loud now.
And your absence is so present.
I can't even breathe.
Sometimes I choke on the tears
Thinking about how hard
The depression made it
For us.
So, forgive me.

For not knowing

Or thinking

That I could've saved you.

I miss you.

Issa Woman, I Think

In the beginning it was just me.
No crown, no money
Just me.
And I'm still learning that
That's enough

That I'm enough.
That what I'm doing is enough.
But the God in Me
Is like Nah.
You don't belong here baby girl.
Every day I wake up
And I'm in the wrong space
The wrong place
At the wrong pace.
I feel the plans
Unraveling.
Promises of a
Happiness I've never felt
But I know exists
I guess
Whenever I'm ready to leave.
The world will be waiting for me.
For this woman
Finally, about to take
Her first steps.

God is a Sister

Who heard your cries and knew
That you needed her.

For Colored Girls Who

Are considering death please
Talk to somebody.

Little Boys & Girls
Don't deserve to be martyrs.
They deserve childhood.

You Deserved to Live
Regardless of what they say.
Your black lives matter.

This is For Tamir
A free black boy who was
Murdered for breathing.

This is For Trayvon
The Mike's, Sandra's, and Tee Tee's

You all deserved more.

Know Justice

If we knew Justice.
You would know Peace.
We wouldn't have families
Broken into pieces
Because of how the police...
polices.
Pleases. Everyone else
But the people they serve.
The people they protect
Are defenseless.
We fight back by reflex.
Little boys playing with fire.
They learn. They live.
They never do it again.
Police forces are not little boys.
Police forced to treat toys, little black boys...
playing with toys like
Animals.
They build lies out of the truth.
But we're brutes?
They saw danger in a 12-year-old baby
Holding a toy.
Playing in the park.
With fire.
And they fired.
Justice put him out.
And we're forced to
deal with the embers.

So...here's a love letter to Justice.
You playing with the wrong fire.
You don't bear the scars
But you will.
Keep playing.
And we will treat you
Like you deserve to be treated.

Laquan

Breathing life into the struggle
By taking your last breath
Not on purpose
But there was a purpose?
No.
I don't want you to be a martyr.
Be a teenager.
Make the wrong choices
Correct them.
That's what life is.
Why does this keep happening?
These questions. No answers.
Black boys are not lambs
But they are being led to slaughter.
Lead into slaughter.
16 shots of it in fact
No justice. No peace.
Especially when we lay in pieces
On the streets and in crumpled up paper
Bonds too weak to hold us together
A poet can't keep it together.
Torn apart by the enforcers.
Perforated like bullets.
POP, POP, POP!
Should be the sound of a binder
Or some pop rocks, or pencils
Making a beat.
But it's just another black boy getting shot.
Ain't no future for a black child in my womb.
When this world likes to make itself
Their first tomb.

These Roots are Deep

I've got Africa hanging from my neck
And I've got black men
For branches.
These roots are endless.

I have the whole world in my hands
And finally I could breathe.
Said the father holding his daughter.
Who didn't know he couldn't breathe before her.

I gave birth to the world.
My daughter.
Showed me how to break
My own chains.
Said the Mother.

I learned what freedom was.
Freedom is a black girl
Unafraid to be herself.
Freedom is a little black girl
Allowed to experience childhood.
Freedom is amazing.
Grace to see that others aren't there yet.
Freedom is love.
It's not boastful
It is kind.
Once you have it
You can't let go.
Once it's in her mind.
She dreams of nothing else.

Sticks and Stones

Your words are bullets,
and your mouth is the trigger
That left me dying

Clean Sweep

There was something in the dust.
Pretty sure I'm going crazy.
But I saw it.
It wasn't smiling.
It wasn't frowning.
It was just there.
Accepted its fate as just something to be.
But I saw it.
I saw it for what it was.
A Man.
A Woman.
A People.
Nomads.
Whose journey has to pick up whenever
Someone deems them unclean.
Whitewash the neighborhoods.
Clean off the table.
Only one group can eat.
But that dust.
It gathers.
While They eat.
He gathers.
Himself.
I saw a face in the dust.
And it looked like mine.
Footprints in the sand.
We keep moving.
But they seem to forget
We always leave roots.
Even after we are long gone.
We are still cracking your pavement.
Reminding you.
These dust free neighborhoods.
Aren't meant to be.

Conversation

Let's talk.
I need to talk.

I want to tell you
About my breakdowns.

Is that selfish of me?

To want to talk
About my problems
Even though this is us.
This uncertainty.
Inner dilemmas
And inner demons
You can't pray away.
We pop pills
To fix it
Ain't no gauze
For depression.
But maybe it'll stop me
From exploding today.
It'll hold me together
Patch these frayed nerves.

I've broken down this week.
More times than I can count.

I'm a little teacup.
Short and stout
Tip me over.
I'm spilling out.
Doesn't make sense.
Right?
Exactly

That'll Be Enough
(inspired by Hamilton and Lemonade)

I look for inspiration
In your eyes.
Only to see my face.
I wish I was enough.
But I just see me.
Not knowing that what I see
In your eyes is your heart.
My reflection is you
I don't get it
I don't understand
But I'm praying
That we fall together.
I don't want to be caught.
Praying you catch me
Dreaming.
It won't be that easy.
falling into our desires.
Freedom tastes like dishonesty.
I'm my own inspiration.

I wonder if our souls share secrets
When we're not watching.
Whispering our destinies
Into existence.
I pray I catch you whispering.
We will be listening.
For an opportunity to become whole.
Kissing spirits
High on the thoughts
Of how you know my
Secrets.
I'm not at ease
Even though this is easy.

Strength

I've been thinking
About laying these burdens down

because
I don't know
If I can do this anymore.

Be black.
Be soft.
Be woman.
Be alive.

We are "known"
For this.
For this untouchable
Unattainable strength.
Sometimes we are vilified
But they don't realize
There is truth to the word.
What don't kill us
Makes us stronger.
And we are strong enough

To mourn.
To feel pain.
To cry.

It takes a strength unknown
To let yourself go.

To remember it's ok
To remember that this,
This hurt. Is ok.

We are our own villages.
And still. It takes a village of us.

To thrive.
You are here.
You are resilient.
You are strength embodied.
We are here.
We are resilient.
We are strength embodied.

Strength

Is

She.

S.I.S

We It.

For black girls
Who's cups are **overflowing**
Cracking

From not being able to contain themselves
I am willing to mend you with shards of myself.
I am broken too.
But pieces of me hold the gold

Strength II

There are women who
grow into broken girls from
promises too big

For her to carry.
When this village of us
Fix you
The things you keep
May be the same
But the inside of you
Will be stronger.
Forged with the strength
Of a thousand black girls.
The village is you.
For the black girls
Who need to break
But there's nobody to
Tend to you.
After you've mended
Everyone.
If You were a broken teacup
I would be the saucer
That catches you.
Don't be afraid to shatter.
Black girl.
I may get cut.
But I want to pick you up.
Put you back together.

Finding Our Girls

I don't think
I ever took a moment
To cry for she.
Me.
Black girl lost
And the only one looking
Is she.
Me.
The only one who knew
The black girl was missing was
Me.
She.
Her.
I.

Never we.

We Find Joy

In the souls
Of the ink.
The same ink
That claimed us.
That we used to steal
That gave us freedom
And took it away
There is joy
In the cursive
Cursed words
Of this woman's pen.
I find joy
Etched onto the skin
Of my brother's keeper.
Who remembered not
Being allowed to
Write so much
That He got the
Words put on him
We are free.
This ink knows it
This skin knows it
I bear my freedom papers.
I dare you to take it.

Chapter 3

Winter is Coming

This may feel like a poem
But it's a love story.
For the girls who want to
Be paid for their work
But the accounts are overdrawn.
Morally bankrupt
And PayPal won't help.
For the girls who
Want love
But only find it in forbidden places.
For the girls who find comfort
In their own tears
The only embrace they've felt in years
Was saltwater trying to
Wash away the pain
That spilled it.
For the girls who find solitude
To be a love song
They're not willing to share.
I don't know what to say.
For the girls who deserve more
But always get less.
I'm not sure
You already have your riches.
For the sisters who
Need love.
I wish my Love was enough.

For the People

Who claim to be colorblind
Who say they don't care
If you were born
With white stripes
And polka dots
All these otherworldly hues.
They sure don't mind
Seeing the red
When it comes to the white and the blue.
They act like they don't see
Color
But are quick to judge
The brown and the black hues.
You don't see color
But you support the blue.
For the ones that say
"It should not be Black Lives Matter,
When only black lives
Are in the front
Being gunned down
In a war we didn't sign up for.
For the people
Who are blinded by
Blue Lights of justice
Shielded by patriotism
Let me tell you what they don't look like.
Since you're so blind.
Justice does not look like
A windfall.

Justice does not look like
opportunities,
And 'GoFundMes'
Created in your name
After you created a victim.
Justice does not look like
An exclusive club
For the people wearing white.
And patriotism does not
Look like a confederate flag
Or an American flag
Being waved in the face
Of people
Sacrificing everything to be
What we're supposed to be.
Equal.
It don't look like that.
If you weren't so caught up
In seeing the made-up colors
Of the imaginary people
You'd treat more fairly
Than the colorful ones already here.
You'd probably see
the black people spilling
The red after being shot by the whites
Wearing the blue.

We so damn patriotic.

"That's Not Our Name"
(3 Haikus)

1. We walk like weapons.
Bringing bodies to gunfights
We already lost.

2. They call us weapons
But act surprised when we bring
bodies to a gunfight

3. Label us weapons
And get mad when we become
Who you thought we were.

Black Girl Prayer

I was born of Southern Fruit
Suffered under white supremacy
Was crucified
And my blood is still being spilt
Our story sounds so much like

Our savior
It's a wonder people don't worship us.
They read our story every Sunday
Using the bible as instructions
Not to leave earth.
But to make us less equal
If we are like Jesus
I wonder if they expect God's forgiveness.
For the ills they've done.
Religion is a funny thing.
It's up for interpretation.

Trigger Warning

It's cold outside.

Don't forget your coat.
You got your bookbag?

Lunch Money?

Alright, give me a kiss.
Have a good day today baby.

That's what my grandma.
My heart.
Tells me every day.
She loves me more
Than I love myself.
And...you know,
At least someone loves me.

Walking to school

Ain't nothing new.
Ain't nothing dangerous
About books, and uniforms.
Right?

Walking to school.

Ain't nothing new.
Ain't nothing dangerous
About books and uniforms.
Until you're
Booked by uniforms.
But they
Ain't supposed to be
Dangerous either.

I was just walking to school.

Sir.
Let me go, or I'm going to be late.
I wish
Better late than never would've chose me today.
But an officer saw me.
Walking to school...

Nothing new...
Cause ain't nothing dangerous
About books and uniforms.
I thought.
I must be some kind of criminal.
I must have done something.
To be shot in the street
For doing something normal.

I'm just trying to get to school.

My grandma told me
I could be anything in the world
If I'm respectful.
If I wear the right clothes.
Carry the right books.
Talk the right talk.
But I can't change my color.
I could've been anything in the world.
My grandma told me.
The police showed me otherwise.
But my grandma told me.
I'm to be mindful of the ways
Of the people you treat.
And you can be anything
You want to be.
In this world.
Not My Baby.
I heard my heart say
Who would hurt her like this.
She didn't deserve this.
I just wanted the best for her.
Anything in the world
For her to be

And the police turn her into
A dead girl on the street.

When my grandma told me
To reach for the clouds.
We didn't expect
The cops would put me there.

Black Boys

These men.
These boys.
Who are we to tell them
They can't hang
Not with their boys
And especially from branches
Black boys hung out so much
You'd think their roots
Were nooses.
What a nuisance.
That strange fruit
The lord seems to never
Get full
Of black boys
Hanging from poplar trees
Swinging in that southern breeze.
How sweet are your
Grandmothers roots.
The white man knows
They knew how to pick them
Ripe with strength
Hung them out to dry
Another nigger ready
For anything...cause hell on earth
Wasn't bad enough.
I wonder if the end of the gun
Is the new noose.
Black boys are lying in the streets
The new fruit

The Three Eyed Raven

The tree speaks for itself

Blood leaks from my leaves
I am a witness
I watch them leave
As death falls upon
My new limb.

Smiles on their faces
Whilst I am burdened
This weight breaks my bough.
This sorrow rocks me
To my roots.

Pale faces watch me
In the moonlight.
As I stare back at them.
I will never forget this sorrow
I will never forget the sparrow.
The owls questioning
The nature of these beasts.
Blood leaks from my leaves
To my roots.
And we are connected.
The forest never forgets.

Africa Has a Voice

I know the blood of my children.
I've felt their bodies crying
Whenever that whip
Kissed their skin
Like the sun did
I felt their pain.
And all I wanted to do
Was hold you.
I used to beg the Gods to
Bury you within me
So you would finally feel
Just how much I loved you
So, you would feel loved at all
I wish I could show you
What you are destined to be
Once free.
Trapped and strapped
And tied up.
They used those trees
Against you.
Unknowingly
they turned my children into seeds
not knowing
How you rise.
How you are destined to grow
From the soils of black folk.
They took you away
But I still feel you.
I always will.

More than one could imagine.
I dream of home.

Rage

I am not surprised.
I am angry.
How do you put rage into words?
There's a burning hatred.
And I'm trying not to burn myself.
To the police.
Fuck you.
To the silent ones.
Fuck you.
To the system.

Fuck you.

To the ppl
Who can't fathom
Why we are becoming
Who were meant to be.

Fuck you.

We are warriors.
We are magic.
We are strength.
We are unforgiving.
We remember.
We see you.
We are your downfall.
The more you kill us.
The more you awaken us.
I am not here for white tears.
I am here for the revolution.
We have nothing to lose
But our chains.
We are already losing our lives.

Riot Postcards

I received a letter in my email
Today.
Little did I know
It would be a picture of
My boy.
Here lies another Emmet Till
'Till equality do us part
Married to a struggle
We shouldn't have to fight for
How many times
How many times
How many times
Must the revolution be socialized.
Black Death
Met by protests
Hashtag solidarity
How many times
Does Trayvon have to die
For you to figure out
He didn't murder himself
How many videos do
We have to watch to
Understand
How many camera phones
have to go live
Before we realize
We're watching
Modern day
Riot Postcards.

Thinking Out Loud

Would we call this a freestyle
In text form?

Just going through some thoughts.

Am I enough
Are we enough
What are we then?
I've been told to go deeper
But any deeper
And I'll lose.

Myself.

I only skim the surface
Because of the comfort.
I can float.
What do we do when we sink
And we can't swim
Out of our thoughts.
I'm scared of getting
Lost in translation
Out at sea
With nobody but me.
I may not be able
To rescue myself.
At least I might be free.

The Hate You Must Have

In your heart
To kill a person.

How angry must you be
To kill a nigger.

A human.
A black people.

Who told you
That you were better.

Who told you that
You were God on earth.

You don't decide.
Who gets to live.

You don't have
That authority over me.

The more things change.
The more they remain the same.

But we ain't never been docile.
That ain't change.

This is an ode to Till.
Little bro you not alone
No more.

You got Trayvon,
And Mike.
And more Trayvons.
And Mikes.

Your deaths
Killed the slaves in us.

Y'all woke up the giant.
Thinking violence would
Intimidate us.

You almost succeeded in eliminating us.
But we are a new generation.
Of giants.

And there is no David
That will take us down.

This is not pride.
This is a truth
That I have known for
Some time now.

Rhythm

When did I get like this.
When did it take
Losing myself in this music
To finally find myself.
Turn the bass up I can feel
Something more powerful

Than my pain

When the beat dropped
I could finally breathe.
If you are the rhythm
I am the Blues.
If I am your music
I wonder who will comfort
You... once I break.
I wonder if your silence
Is as painful as mine was
And I wonder if your pain
Comforted you
Like the ad libs on this record.
I wonder
If I'm your music
Who's recording us.

Krystal Kantrell

Chapter 4

Blossom, Black Girl

Black Girl
So delicate
She breaks apart
Even when
She's got it together
On the outside
Looking in
I feel you slipping
Let me catch you
Before you fall
I can hold your weight
You are not a burden
But I choose to carry you.
I want to.
Your heart is the heaviest
But my strength
Is prepared
To give you everything
You didn't know
You needed.

Baby Girl

I worry about my daughter
With her cocoa skin
Her almond eyes
Full of wonder
Her kinky hair
A brown halo
My angel
I can't wait to show her
What the world has for her

        I worry about my daughter
        Her alabaster skin
        Curly hair and her blue eyes
        Full of wonder
        I can't wait to show her
        What the world has for her

I fear for my daughter
With her cocoa skin
And her almond shaped eyes
The pain this world has in store for her
The feeling of waiting for the inevitable
A pain like no other
A world that would steal her
and her brothers
With no regrets
No punishments
I should wait to show her
What this world has in store for her.

        I fear for my daughter
        With her fair skin
        And those blue eyes, so trusting

How will she know
What kind of people to trust
I'm not a racist or anything
But I have to teach her who to trust
The police will protect her
She's a good little girl
She'll be ok.
The world is looking out for her.

My brown daughter.
I fear for her
I fear the people who think
She's something to fear
Or people who think she's something
And not some person
Maybe I should wait
Hold her hand a little longer
Wait... don't let go.
I have to teach her who to trust
Her brothers will look out for her
I hope
But who will look out for them?
The Kings.
I fear this world
Will take our power
They twist our lives
Turn them into lies
I fear for my blackness.
Maybe I will wait
Just a little while longer
To have my daughter.
Because what this world
Clearly has in store...
I'll never be ready for.

Love Notes

Sometimes...

I just wanna write you

Love notes
Because you deserve them.

I Just wanna send you

A text to tell you

How beautiful you are
To me.

Sometimes...

I just want to

Let my fingers do the talking with you.

Actually,
Love.

Ever since I saw your wings
I've wondered if your feathers
Would feel like freedom.

On a Good Day

I'll forget that things aren't
Hopeless.
I'll remember that I'm still here.
And that
You can still hear me
Even though you're not listening.
On a good day.
I'll forget that the notes
I write in my head
equal up to chapter books.
And that the only reader is the author.
On a good day
I'll thank God
For giving me the demons
That stop me from
Wanting any days at all.
On a good day.
I'll forget the faded scars
I created to relieve
My own pressure.
Still bursting at the seams.
My mind
Feels like a balloon
Ready to pop most days.
But on a good day.
Hopefully
I'll forget who I am
And crack a real smile
And maybe let someone
Get to me
Before I do.
On a good day
I hope that someone feels me
when I no longer
Feel myself.

Cranes in The Sky

I just wish I couldn't feel it.

I'm **desperate.**

But how do you
Survive your escape
From this life.

Away.

From this place.

Cranes in the sky
Are what I aspire to.
Freedom
Is what that
Must be.
Their flight
Must be freedom.

Their closeness
To the clouds.

How Godly they are.
To feel weightless
Of the ways of the world
Must be how freedom feels.

Weary

Why
We gotta
Be like this.
Why
We gotta
Be strong.
Why
Can't we be tired.
Let me give up
Just for a second.
And I'll pick it back up.
That's not us.
Black girl.
Get yourself together.
Be ready.
Be better.
Weary or not.
Weary for naught.
I'm so tired.
But I'm going
To find my
Glory.
The one that resides
In me.
I belong here.
It only took a small
Trip to the heart
Of the matter
To figure things out.

Rise

Aye girl

                     That mistake you made
                             Yesterday.

Leave it.

Make a new one.

A better one today.

                            Fix it tomorrow.

Cause we gonna get it.

It'll take some time.
We got it.
Fall in your ways.
So you can sleep.

                      And rise in the morning.

Cause Sis.
New mistakes
Got our names
All over them.

Living Art

I have been bursting.
It took me a while to realize
I am the poem
I've been trying
To write
Mourning memories
I can't seem to remember.
Bursting with words I don't have
Breathe girl.
Exhale those thoughts
Finding pain
I never lost
My body is a piece.
I've been stumbling
Over all these writer's
Blocks.
If my pen would've just
Picked me up sooner
I could've had something
To put back together
A word or 2
Or 3
For me.
I am a living poem.
The way my eyes see
Feelings
"And the way my ears
hear pain I am this haiku
Yet to be written"

Pray You Catch Me

Breathe Girl.
Take your time.
Catch your breath.
Hold on to this moment.
When he showed you
Who he really was
It hurts to breathe right now
I know it does
But you push through.
This is what
Black girls do.
We do this.
This is what we're made for.
Heart Break and Hard times
Everybody ain't able
But we are.
But you are.
We're strong enough.
Breathe.
Whispers to God.
Asking for help.
That hopefully She
Will understand
Why everyone's Rock
Finally needs a bed
To rest.
Stand still for a moment.
Just for a heart beat.
And Let it go.
It's ok to feel human.

Release

I saw my aunt's smile
For the first time
In 15 years
The corners of her lips
Whispered into her ears

Everything is alright

Her dimples used to dip
under the pressure
Of holding diamond mines
Of sadness
Her heart spoke in volumes of

Mama. I'm home

And then they hugged her
15 years
Lifetimes have passed
But we've been waiting
All our lives
For freedom.
I never knew what it felt like
Until I saw it in my cousin's eyes.

Michelle Obama

Black Girl Magic, embodied.
Competition? Where?

Forty-Five Issa

No, nah, not my president.
He can go. He thought.

Lynch

My head is hot.
My throat is sore.
My heart is hurting.
Sometimes I'll ride
In my car
Not realizing I'm driving
And I'll watch the trees.
I wonder if they
Pass on the pain
That they may have held
To passerby's.
Southern Trees
Are singing
In the southern breeze.
They no longer swing
It reminds them of the people.
Man-made swing sets
Man. Made. Swing. Sets.
I used to wonder if death
And southern trees
Greeted each other like old friends.
I hope that the trees
Handled their involuntary
Burdens with care.
I hope that lynched Men
Women
Girls
Boys
Were rocked to sleep
I hope their souls drifted away
Like leaves falling
As the seasons change.
I hope that
Nature showed more humanity
To my people
Than humans.

Georgia On My Mind

All Georgia is
Is cottonfields
And cities who forgot
Where they came from.
The people are the same.
Made up of dirt roads and peanut fields
We've forgotten how to grow.

Our history is the crop
That needs to be sowed.

If we valued ourselves
As much as King Cotton
No gin would be able to keep us.
Running to vices for escape
When

all we need to do
Is to bloom.

Krystal Kantrell

Krystal Kantrell

Meet the Author

Krystal Kantrell

is a poet from Waynesboro, GA, raised in between the cities of
Augusta, GA and Cottageville, SC.

She is a graduate of South Carolina State University and a former
member of The Marching 101 Band. She has lived in black cities
and gone to black colleges all her life.

Her work has been published on the site, 'For Harriet', and she
was the first black female author signed to the BlackGold
Publishing Team. Her work can also be found garnishing praise in
various inboxes of her special friends.

She is only serious when she writes poetry, and tries to find the
silver lining in every situation.
And when she can't find one... she makes one.

Please follow her on Black Twitter: @kryskrossed or on Facebook;
@Krys Kantrell for any further
entertainment or updates on her work.